# Unjunk
# Your Life

50 ways to help you edit your life so that you can
focus on your health and happiness

## Kimberley Durst

**Unjunk Your Life**

ISBN: 978-1-988215-01-3

Editing and Pre-press:
*words along the path*
a branch of One Thousand Trees
www.onethousandtrees.com

*To all the readers who have the courage
to make change in their daily lives by
"unjunking."  Here's to keeping only what
adds value and joy in your life.  Quality of life
begins with the quality of our surroundings,
what we put into and onto our bodies
as well as how we nurture ourselves.*

# Introduction

I'm going to be blunt; junk doesn't belong in your life. Most junk belongs in the proverbial "junkyard." I guarantee that, once it's gone, you won't miss it. By limiting yourself to the essential and clearing away the clutter, you can focus on what's important: your health and happiness. Curating an environment that makes you smile is good for you, and contributes to your overall well-being. Many of us are strangely comforted by "stuff" -- aka "junk" -- so be forewarned that this process of "unjunking" is not necessarily easily done.

Another caveat I will pass on, before you begin the process of unjunking your life, is that any progress is still progress; you'll still be surpassing everyone who will still be sitting on the couch. You don't have to go hard core like the Japanese cleaning guru Marie Kondo. Her housekeeping manual, *The Life-Changing Magic of Tidying Up*, has inspired many to throw away their unneeded belongings. You don't need to do everything all at once. Start with what you feel comfortable with, and according to your timeline. In order to minimize the frustration of it taking too long, I suggest alternating some of the BIG unjunks with smaller unjunks.  The big ones may take weeks, months, heck even years to complete whereas some of the smaller ones can be checked off in a few minutes.  To keep this "unjunked" life a reality, organize a "throwing out" day every month to make sure that you don't have clutter building up.

If you start editing your life as you live it, you will notice that you don't accumulate as much junk.  I urge you to focus on quality rather than quantity.  Our society as a whole has become collectors of stuff.  Many of us assign a value to our lives by how much "stuff" we have.   Once you are empowered to see it for what it is -- junk -- you will be amazed at how much easier it becomes to free yourself.  It's time to KISS.  No, not that kind but if it helps, go ahead.   Keep it simple....silly.  You have one life and one chance to make what you do count; don't waste it on junk.  Investing time to "unjunk" could be the best investment you've ever made; it's an investment in yourself and your happiness.  Start today and don't delay.  You'll be glad you did it now rather than later.   There's a little hoarder in all of us; nip it in the bud.  You don't need more in your life, just better.  The old adage, less is more, really can be true. You will be amazed at how cathartic this can be; I speak from experience: less mess, less stress!

You decide how you want to attack this challenge! Yes, each unjunk is numbered but only because convention dictates that lists have numbers. There is no right way or wrong way as long as you are moving forward. This is a very personal project. It is your prerogative to do it your way! You decide how to approach this mission. Are you the type to read the book from start to finish before you decide where to start? Maybe you're the spontaneous type who flips to a random page and goes for it! Whatever your gut tells you to do: take Nike's advice and just do it! Personally, I like the element of surprise. My husband would definitely read the book from start to finish and would make a spreadsheet to track his progress. See where I'm going with this? It is completely, totally, 100% up to you with no wrong way. The world will not end based on your decision. The only thing that matters is your decision to make it happen! Build in your own rewards as you go. I've tried to help you by providing a space for you to record when you've finished each task. One of my favourite rewards is R & R time: bath bomb anyone? Remember, you are doing this for you! You are done with putting it off for another day, week, month or year (s)!

Here goes your first unjunking. You can do it. You are stronger than you think. Just one more piece of advice; guilt is a useless emotion. If you find yourself too emotionally attached to something, ask yourself some questions like: Why? What can I do to preserve the memories instead of hanging onto the physical evidence? You may wish to delegate some of the process to others if you find yourself unable to complete it for whatever reason. There are resources available to help you. Do not be afraid to call in the big guns ie. 1-800- Got-Junk. Unfortunately, they do not take away emotional junk but do a bang up job getting rid of the physical junk that we all harbour. Another option for junk that could be turned into someone else's treasure is a charity. Many charities accept almost anything provided it is in working condition and clean. By finding inspiration in gratitude and shifting your mindset from lack of abundance to realizing that we have so much, you will feel free to let go of things you don't really need (Buttigieg, 2015). There are no excuses to not do this. Your health and happiness depend on it.

Are you dreaming up ways to procrastinate already? Not to worry; give yourself a few minutes to check email, watch some YouTube videos or call a friend. By giving yourself permission and getting the inevitable out of the way, it will help you tackle the task at hand. Next, get some good music lined up. An upbeat playlist goes a long way in keeping you motivated. If you're still not ready, go for a walk to clear your mind. While out in nature, you may come to the realization that it is doable and not as overwhelming as you first thought. Or you may decide that you need to get some distance. If you could manage a weekend away in a hotel, for example, that taste of what it's like to live in a clutter-free space may be what it takes. When you come back relaxed, renewed and rejuvenated, you will be ready (Buttigieg, 2015).

## Acknowledgments

I would like to acknowledge the love and support from all who had a part in this book: you know who you are.

# 1

Let's get kick-started with a big unjunk : Habits. People are very habitual. There are good habits and not so good habits. I'm positive you can quickly identify which ones are which very easily, without my help. "We are what we repeatedly do," Aristotle proclaimed. Another nugget from Aristotle goes like this: "Excellence…is not an act but a habit." Once you have identified the self-destructive, self-limiting habits that you must junk, you must decide which good habits you will keep as well as which good habits you will add to your daily regimen. I assure you that the longer you stick with it, the greater chance of success.

Date: _____

# 2

You knew that if one thing was making it onto the list, it would definitely be the proverbial junk drawer. Yes, even though it is designed for junk, it still needs a good de-junking every once in a while to make room for the new junk: makes sense!

Date: _____

# 3

Who needs a wardrobe with sizes ranging from small to x-large? Another fashion faux pas is thinking it will come back into fashion; while this may be true, will you still be able to pull it off? Donate all the clothes you haven't worn in the past year and free up the space for some new digs. Conversely, don't buy anything new and your choices in the morning will be easier with fewer items to critique.

Date: _____

# 4

When you're done with the clothes, move on to the other closets in the house. For example, your linen closet. Think of all the people who could be actually using your old blankets and sheets for their intended purpose. We all think that some time down the road, we will suddenly have a need to use all this extra bedding: wrong! You will feel so much better when you can open and close the door without an avalanche!

Date: _____

# 5

Are you or aren't you having another baby? If the answer is a definitive no, then you are good to go. Obviously, if you are not sure, you may want to hang onto all the baby paraphernalia. If you're waiting for your sister to decide, now that's another story. Look, if she still hasn't found the "right" one, let her buy her own nursery. It is not an obligation to hang on to stuff for other people in the hope that they may need it. If your baby has grown into an individual that could be coerced into helping with these tasks, perfect. An extra set of hands, no matter how small, can really be beneficial. You may want to encourage them to decide what stays and what goes. A little bribery goes a long way: just saying. You have to do whatever it takes. Who knows what your charming offspring could sell at a garage sale or even a table set up at the end of a driveway?

Date: _____

# 6

TV time: yes, you need to decide if you actually need to watch another episode of reality TV. Really? Go out and make your own reality. It will prove to be more interesting and a better use of your time. If you feel like mindless TV is the only antidote, then at least make the time productive. While you are unwinding, stretch, delete old apps, look for new healthy recipes, throw in a plank or there's my favourite: sort and organize receipts. If you decide to forgo the television, take a hike and in the process unjunk your mind. Take your mind off all of the lists and other mental baggage, and breathe in some forest air. Most of us are walking zombies partially because we are nature deficient. We deprive ourselves of nature and the amazing natural side effects. Studies have shown that getting outside can actually lower your risk of depression and anxiety, or help you if you suffer from those conditions.

Date: _____

# 7

Recipe collection and take-out menus: you might not have a recipe collection per se, but that pile of ripped out magazine recipes could qualify. Are you really sure you might one day get the urge to make homemade anything? I really hope you do but let's face it; you can easily find any recipe you are looking for on the internet: Ditto for take-out menus. Scraps of paper just get in the way and take up space. Scan a digital image instead of keeping the hard copy.

Date: _____

# 8

Cravings need to be unjunked mainly because there is likely some sort of deficiency behind them. Before you try to decipher what the craving means, start with a tall glass of plain water. Most of us are chronically dehydrated and mistake thirst for hunger. If that doesn't do the trick, here are some other reasons:

Chocolate craving: you might be low in magnesium. Try a small piece of dark chocolate to get you past it and then add more nuts, seeds, leafy greens and fish to your diet.

Sweets: you might be experiencing blood sugar fluctuations. A quick fix is a piece of fruit but long-term add more complex carbs and high fibre foods.

Salty: you might be stressed! Try some relaxation techniques like deep breathing and add in more leafy greens and a high-quality B complex vitamin.

Cheese: sometimes indicates a fatty-acid deficiency. Add in some Omega 3s.

Red Meat: you need more iron in your diet. The obvious solution is to add more iron-rich foods such as dried fruit, beans and legumes as well as high-quality meat but not too much (not more than 15% of your total daily diet) (Rosenthal, 2014).

Date: _____

# 9

Cleaning supplies are a biggie. Marketing companies make a fortune selling us the latest and greatest. We are so easily convinced by those infomercials: another reason not to watch too much late night or early morning TV. Stick with the good stuff you already have on hand: baking soda and vinegar. If you want to mask the vinegar aroma, add in a drop or two of some essential oils. Why add more toxic chemicals to your house?

Date: _____

# 10

Do you have a shed that is just crammed to the rafters with junk? You know what I mean: old flower pots, broken lawn furniture, gnomes that have lost their colour and joie de vive? If you did not use it last season, you will likely not use it next season.

Date: _____

# 11

Are you able to park in your garage or are you keeping your junk warm? I know so many people that have a garage that is not being used for the intended purpose. If you are having to scrap the snow and ice off your car just so you don't have to clean out your garage, I think you know what you need to do: pronto!

Date: _____

# 12

Sugar: Try a 10 day sugar cleanse to get unjunked and reset your palate. Once you are able to give it up, you will notice that your cravings subside and you don't miss it like you thought. Even a little sugar causes you to crave more. If you must sweeten up your coffee, tea or baking, stevia is a good alternative.

Date: _____

# 13

Drinks: You need to drink more water and ditch pop, juice and sports drinks. Water makes up your body and regulates all functions of the body. Water gets rid of the junk, aka toxins, in your body. A lot of people are chronically dehydrated. You're not sick or hungry, you're simply thirsty. Herbal teas are another great option since they also have medicinal and nutritional properties (Rosenthal, 2014).

Date: _____

# 14

Career:  Many of us spend eight to ten hours a day doing something we don't really enjoy.  Many people complain about their job but feel powerless to change it.  Unjunk your career by either finding work you love or loving the work you have.  Sometimes it is not possible to go out and create a new career.  Start thinking about what is working and what is not working.  By making a few adjustments in a few key areas, you could make your job more rewarding.  By using good communication skills, you can try to improve the job you have.  It is up to you to ask for what you need. You may be surprised.  If you talk to your boss about leaving and the reasons why, s/he may decide that keeping you is worth a pay increase or more flex time.  Sometimes all you need is a small change to have a renewed appreciation for your job (Rosenthal, 2014).

Date: _____

# 15

Do you have some extra junk in your trunk? Has your exercise regime gone out the window? Movement aids digestion, circulation and respiration. You don't necessarily have to go out and buy an expensive gym membership. Outdoor exercising can be an opportunity to reconnect with nature. Parks are a great place, especially early morning before the parade of toddlers. There are monkey bars to boot! There are endless exercises that can be done in the comfort of your own home that you don't need equipment for. Start exercising away the extra junk.

Date: _____

# **16**

Could your finances use some unjunking? One of the most difficult topics is money. Seek out help if this area even if it's your forté. An outside perspective or new outlook is needed from time to time. Ask friends who are doing well for referrals. Notice that I didn't say ask family. Your business is your business.

Date: _____

# 17

Unjunk your breakfast and you will be more satisfied the rest of the day, and have fewer cravings. Your brain craves high calorie foods when you skip breakfast. This is why individuals who have maintained a significant weight loss one year or longer are breakfast eaters. Egg eaters lose more weight than bagel eaters (Vanderwal et al., 2008).

Date: _____

# 18

Spices: If you're like me, I only rarely use the vast array of exotic spices I have on hand. I have good intentions to find new recipes but I never seem to get to that point. They are so old that they probably don't even have any potency to them. I don't think they go bad per se but seriously; unjunk your spices and be done with it once and for all. Going forward, buy what you will make use of and in limited quantities.

Date: _____

# 19

Unjunk the wheat from your diet and you will experience a transformation. The wheat today is not the wheat we used to eat. Modern wheat contains an altered form of the protein, gliadin, which is an opiate. Rather than providing pain relief like other opiates, the gliadin causes addictive eating behaviour, food obsessions, and increased calorie intake. Another problem is that modern wheat contains 9x the gluten and the structure has changed so it is difficult to digest. Lastly, it is very inflammatory and inflammation is at the core of most disease conditions (Davis, 2014).

Date: _____

# 20

Medicine cabinet: I am convinced that most of us have expired medicine in our homes. Not only should you not be using it but it also poses a risk if the wrong person gets a hold of it. It is not fit to be consumed; the only option is to throw it out. Before you just junk it, you may wish to take the "junk" medicine to your neighbourhood pharmacy so they can dispose of it properly. We don't need any more junk in our water system. Some over-the-counter medications can be replaced with natural substitutions. For example, herbs such as ginger and turmeric are good at reducing inflammation. Tums or Pepto-bismol can be trumped by ginger teas or digestive enzymes. If you experience indigestion, try swallowing 1 Tbsp of apple cider vinegar. When it comes to the cold and flu, you need to support your body's ability to fight infection. Echinacea, goldenseal, oil of oregano and zinc tablets do just that. For nasal congestion, try using a neti pot or steam infused with eucalyptus oil. If you have a teenager in the house, you probably have acne remedies. Pimples need minerals, not chemicals. At bedtime, dab sole water onto each blemish. Sole water is made by putting 2-3 Himalayan salt rocks in a glass jar and filling with water. Let it sit overnight and keep in a jar for daily use. For minor cuts and scrapes keep tea tree oil, manuka honey, and oil of oregano on hand. Manuka honey is also good for applying to burns as it speeds healing and prevents infection (Worts, 2014).

Date: _____

# 21

CDs, DVDs, Floppy Disks – any of them that you don't use or haven't used for months are ready to be junked! If you simply can't part with them, at least take them out of their cases and find a storage system that can be put away for you to pull out again and use....never. In a pinch, you could use them as coasters.

Date: _____

# 22

Most of us over time have accumulated a lot of superfluous holiday decorations. Amidst the good ones, I know there are ones that don't quite cut it anymore. Next time the holiday decorations come out, put away half and donate the other half. Giving is the best feeling, especially when you can give to a charity that can repurpose it for someone else to enjoy. Don't be a Grinch.

Date: _____

# 23

Can't muster up the courage to throw out old documents? Lucky for us, we have the power to scan and store them electronically for posterity without the junk clutter. Paper takes up valuable real estate. The best part about electronic storage is you don't really see it! Yes, there is an app out there that will scan your paper and keep a copy for as long as you need.

Date: _____

# 24

You may believe that at some point in the future, near or far, you will summon the urge to pick up that racquet and go play a game of squash. Really? Let's be honest. If you haven't used a piece of sporting equipment in years, donate it so someone else can get their game on. FYI: Old stationary bikes and treadmills are not meant to be used as drying racks.

Date: _____

# 25

Unjunk and upgrade your alcohol cabinet. At some point in time, I'm sure you've been the recipient of a liquid gift that is not what you're accustomed to. There it sits waiting patiently until your teenage kids decide that you'll never miss it. Get rid of it so that it doesn't continue to taunt them, and you can replace it guilt free with a libation you enjoy.

Date: _____

# 26

We all could use an unjunking of our motivation. It's time to think about what your intentions are and what is the motivation to get there. Are you motivated for the right reasons? This exercise could take a while. Please don't rush it. It's not like earlier tasks such as the junk drawer. You have to go DEEP. Silence and solitude may be required.

Date: _____

# 27

Have you been reading labels? If not, start looking through your snack cupboard. How much sugar is in your snacks? Are there ingredients you can't pronounce? Aim for snacks with less than 10g of sugar and 5 or less ingredients. If it does not meet the above criteria, you need to junk it!

Date: _____

# 28

Are you nourishing yourself in healthy ways? Unjunking your life begins with taking good care of yourself. By unjunking your self-care rituals, you will find yourself feeling happier, healthier and more balanced. This means examining what your habits include. Instead of reaching for ice cream or wasting time on social media, grab a good book, run a bath with essential oils or Epsom salts and, voilà, new you!

Date: _____

# 29

Old makeup is a breeding ground for bacteria. Throw out the old and treat yourself to some new colours. It is about keeping you healthy and looking your best. There are programs out there that let you recycle your makeup, such as MAC, which lets you exchange six empty containers for a new eyeshadow, lip gloss, or lipstick.

Date: _____

# 30

Did you inherit your grandmother's encyclopedia set? Books that are no longer relevant, or that you can easily access electronically, can be filed under J for Junk. Why keep old books? They just smell up your house; mold and mildew are common problems with old books. Time to focus on editing your library. Your children may do it for you if you wait long enough but there might be a bit of resentment. They won't want to spend their precious time throwing out your old junk; trust me, been there and done that. Another option is to try and sell the books if you think they are worth the time and effort. You could even trade them for something else on a swap site; just don't trade for more junk!

Date: _____

# 31

Still planning on creating beautiful scrapbooks of all your family holidays? I have a suggestion: no cutting or gluing required when you make your scrapbooks online. They will bind it and the quality looks professional no matter what your ability; unlike the traditional route. Donate your supplies to a school or camp. It is a great activity to keep kids busy but you, my friend, have better things to do with your time.

Date: _____

# 32

Imagine having an up-to-date address book and contact list? I know it is hard to fathom such a simple yet hard-to-do concept. Instead of using your address book to hold scraps of paper with updated addresses, you can use it alphabetically! Why not just go electronic and be done with it? I know you want to. Another bonus is that you can easily edit people out of your life too, if you choose to.

Date: _____

# 33

 Relationships: romantic and other.  If you have any relationships that are bringing you down, it's time to put an end to them.  You know the kind I'm talking about; the "friend" who uses you constantly when it's convenient for them but is never there for you.  You will feel relieved and will spend more time on your "healthy" relationships instead of fretting over the "unhealthy" ones.

Date: _____

# 34

Friends come in all different shapes, sizes and personalities. If your personality does not jive with someone else, you don't have to be friends. Unlike family, you get to choose your friends. You can also choose the level of friendship. If you're not ready to completely get rid of a "frenemy" you can choose to not really spend time with them; if you keep putting them off, eventually they will move on.

Date: _____

# 35

There is a little hoarder lurking in all of us. Many of us have grown up in a household with lots of knick knacks, clutter etc. Newsflash – you do not have to live the same way as your parents did. Guilt is a useless emotion. When asked about Great Edna's china plate, I am confident that you can come up with a completely plausible explanation as to why you no longer have it: get creative.

Date: _____

# 36

How many shoes does a person wear on any given day? Let us say that you need gym shoes to work out, business shoes to go to work in, casual shoes for running errands, dress up shoes for funerals, weddings etc. and times that by four seasons; I am being generous. If you have more than 16 pieces of footwear, you should consider how happy you could make someone with holes in their shoes when you donate what you truly do not need. Oprah Winfrey in her book What I Know For Sure freely admits that she has too many shoes. In order to be "lean and clean for the future, [she is going to] dust off her wings so it's easier to fly. Enough already with the stuff that doesn't enhance who we really are. That's the real deal of decluttering, a process that's ever evolving as you move closer to the self you were meant to be. And saying good-bye to too many shoes is a darn good start."

Date: _____

# 37

We all know the saying that if something is not broken, do not fix it. However, if it is broken, you should junk it. Speaking from experience, the longer it sits broken, the less likely it will ever be fixed.

Date: _____

# 38

Did you stay up late watching infomercials and now have a drawer full of kitchen gadgets that you never use? Me too! Other than being great conversation starters when you're hosting a party, they really need to find another home. Other kitchen unjunks include: plastic Tupperware from before 2010 because it contains BPA which is a very dangerous, hormone disrupting chemical, scratched non-stick pans and your kitchen sponge. A University of Arizona study found that a typical kitchen sponge is 200,000 times dirtier than a toilet seat. OMG! A friend of mine passed on a great strategy for figuring out what you need and what you don't. Start by putting all your kitchen gadgets, Tupperware and small devices into a box. As you need these items, take them out and once finished with them, do not put them back into the box but rather find a spot for them in the kitchen. At the end of the month, whatever is left in the box is clearly not being used and can be donated.

Date: _____

# 39

All fat is not created equally. There are good fats that our body needs and uses as an energy source. Then there are the bad kinds that could be lurking in your cupboard unbeknownst to you. Unjunk the following fat: hydrogenated, trans fat.

Date: _____

# 40

The last time I went to use sprinkles for cupcake topping, they came out of the container in one massive lump. This is not the way sprinkles should come out! Once in a while, like yearly, one should unjunk their baking supplies so that when in a pinch, you have edible ingredients.

Date: _____

# 41

Feeling like you are low in good spirit? This happens to all of us from time to time. Think about unjunking your mental well-being with activities that make you feel grateful. Often a phone call to a friend that is long overdue will do the trick. Another way is to get or give a good hug. Oxytocin is released when we touch another person. Most of us are touch deprived as well. Go get what you need to feel better. Fake it until you make it.

Date: _____

# 42

Betcha didn't know that most of us have a pH that is out of balance. Most people who suffer from unbalanced pH are acidic. Mild acidosis can lead to a wide variety of problems, from kidney stones to low energy, and even a greater risk of cancer. How do you fix this? First test your urine in the morning with a strip of pH paper and compare the colour on the strip with the chart on the package. Try to do this a few days in a row to see if your pH is consistent. If your pH is lower than 6.4, it is a call to action. You can unjunk your pH in a few ways: drink more water and reduce or eliminate refined, processed, calorie-dense foods. Increase your intake of vegetables, most fruits and sea vegetables, bone broth and coconut water (Jacks, 2014).

Date: _____

# 43

Take a stroll to your bathroom and find out if your shampoo, conditioner, lotions etc. contain these harmful, chemical ingredients: Ammonium lauryl sulfate, sodium laureth sulfate, sodium chloride, polyethelyne glycol, parabens, formaldehyde and lanolin, petroleum, and mineral oil. When you do your research, you will see why these ingredients should not be used. They are not good for you or your body so in other words, they are junk.

Date: _____

# 44

Protein sources vary widely and some are better than others. One of the reasons is the food your food is eating. That was not a typo. When your food source is being given hormones and antibiotics as well as being grain fed versus grass fed, it affects the quality of your protein. Choose clean protein whenever feasible and junk the rest. If you are a meat eater, start by buying a portion of your meat that is grass fed and free of antibiotics as well as hormones.

Date: _____

# 45

"Happiness is an inside job." – Mandy Hale

Your attitude is a choice. It is the glass half full or half empty dilemma. We are in control of our attitude and ensuing happiness. Yes, speed bumps are inevitable; even potholes may surprise us occasionally on the journey of life. How you choose to deal with these hard times makes a big difference. If you let problems define you, you will have a harder time solving them and moving forward. You may also want to investigate the connection between junk food and a junk mood. Another trigger is seeing your house full of clutter. It can affect your mood negatively and make your personal space seem like a place you want to run from.

Date: _____

# 46

Adrenal glands need to be unjunked because they are the masters of your stress hormones and stress response. Modern day living is stressful, agree? Along with day-to-day stress, eating poorly is another stress that wreaks havoc on your body. In fact, 60% of a person's stress comes from diet. (Jacks, 2014) How do you unjunk this area? Well, simply put you must implement a proper diet, sleep, relax and find ways to show your body you care about it.

Date: _____

# 47

Unjunking your digestive system is important for so many reasons. For one, this system is responsible for accessing the nutrients that your body needs. I have to mention flatulence otherwise I'll never hear the end of it from my kids. If you suffer from a lot of gas, your digestive system is probably in distress and needs to be unjunked. When my house starts to get stinky, I know we need to do some tweaking in the area of digestion. Again, it starts with what you're eating or not eating. Ginger and lemon are great digestive aids which make a wonderful tea. You also need enough fibre as well as sufficient hydration. Good fats are also a must, as well as probiotic bacteria. Naturally fermented foods are great sources.

Date: _____

# 48

A lot of people I meet wish for one thing: a faster metabolism. They think that if that were the case, they could eat anything they wanted and not gain weight. I hate to be the bearer of bad news, but they are still working on that magic bullet. However, there are ways to unjunk your metabolism in order to heal it so it will run efficiently, the way it did when you were a kid. A way to do this includes the same advice I keep coming back to: eat a balanced diet of mostly plants. Another strategy that will save you time at the gym is to switch from hours of cardio to lots of weights and HIIT. What the heck is HIIT, you ask? High Intensity Interval Training is an exercise strategy that alternates periods of short intense anaerobic exercise with less intense recovery periods. As you build muscle, you are using energy all day long. HIIT workouts are excellent because they are high intensity. You use way more energy because of the intensity and, again, you use more energy long after the workout is done.

Date: _____

# 49

We live in a consumer society and are always adding to our material possessions. Yes, there are needs and wants but time and time again, the line is blurred. Take time to figure out for yourself what material possessions you truly need and which ones may have been bought on a whim. Are there things you bought that you thought would bring you happiness when in fact they just weigh you down? If you have material possessions that are worth something and you could benefit from the extra cash, there are many ways to make that happen. By unjunking the things in our life that we don't truly need, we tend to see more clearly what we have already that we haven't appreciated as much as we could. By gaining more margin in different areas of your life, you tend to feel in control and, as a result, clarity is able to surface. Oprah Winfrey says in her book What I Know For Sure that she has decided to keep only that which delights her or enhances her well-being. She also quotes organizational expert Peter Walsh who has written the book Enough Already. He believes that our homes are "overwhelmed with stuff and [our] lives littered with the empty promises that the stuff didn't fulfill…In buying what we want, we hope to acquire the life we desire…[But] chasing the life you want by accumulating more stuff is a dead-end street." I agree with Oprah when she says "Cleaning house – both literally and metaphorically – is a great way to hit the Refresh button."

Date: _____

# 50

We have the power to change our life by changing our thoughts. Negative thoughts can not only weigh you down and prevent you from reaching your potential but can actually change the trajectory of your life. When we evaluate our thoughts and toss out the junk ones, we are left with the good. What we do and become is partially because of what we think and what we give power to. Try to catch yourself or others when they are being "Negative Nellies" and call them out on it. If you're habitually negative, life tends to stay that way. Look for any silver lining you can because it could always be worse.

Date: _____

# 51

Bonus: your choice! What have I forgotten? I know there is still something that you need to eliminate from your life. Congratulations on putting this book to work. No matter how long it took you or even how well you completed certain tasks, you did it. Did I mention that this is a journey? You may have reached your destination for now, but I implore you to keep going. Only you know what you have to do to live your best life possible. Go and make it happen.

Date: _____

# Conclusion

I truly hope that you have gotten out of this book what you need. It will be different for every reader. No doubt, some of you will have each of the fifty tasks dutifully accounted for and dated. Others may find that they really only needed to do a few of the most important ones. Then there are others still who will have every intention to keep going back over time to complete a few more. It is your book and it is your prerogative. The same can be said for your journey to health; it is up to you. It is your choice. You get to decide what your priorities are. You get to decide on the timeline. Only you can make it happen. Go for it.

# References

Intro
• Buttigieg, H. "Get Motivated"
Homedigest, Late Spring 2015 Ontario Edition

#19
• Davis, W. "Wheat Belly Total Health"
Canada: Haper Collins Publishers Ltd., 2014.

#20
• Worts, S. "Make-over your medicine cabinet"
Escarpment Magazine, Spring 2014.

#45
• Jacks, J. "Discover the Power of Food" Canada:
Romarah Inc., 2014.

#8    #13    #14
• Rosenthal, J. "Integrative Nutrition"
New York: Greenleaf Book Group LLC., 2014.

#17
• Vanderwal, J.S. et al. Egg breakfast enhances
weight loss. International Journal of Obesity:
Published online August 2008.